The Art of **DreamWorks**

THE BOSS BABY

Written by Ramin Zahed

FOREWORD BY
Alec Baldwin

PREFACE BY
Tom McGrath

AFTERWORD BY
Marla Frazee

TITAN BOOKS

London
An Insight Editions Book

Contents

Foreword

by Alec Baldwin

I've played a lot of tough-talking, coffee-swilling business executives throughout my career, but I have to admit none of them can hold a pacifier to the diaper-wearing boss I play in DreamWorks Animation's latest movie. Having been born the first of four boys and having four children of my own, I know a thing or two about what happens when a new baby arrives in a household and steals the spotlight from you. That's why I couldn't resist voicing the part of Boss Baby.

What is truly remarkable about this movie is how it captures the reality of what it's like to deal with a new sibling in a family, all the while providing a barrage of whimsical humor, imagination, and pure heart. To top it off, the brilliant animators at DreamWorks have created a computer-animated movie that pays tribute to some of my favorite classic cartoons and movies we all grew up with.

I was so impressed by the meticulous world created by the film's director Tom McGrath, producer Ramsey Naito, and the rest of their talented team. So much attention has been paid to each character design, piece of background art, line of dialogue, effect, and piece of music. However, when we experience the movie as a whole, we are immersed in a parallel world that looks vaguely familiar but unlike anything else we've seen before on the big screen.

In the movie, Boss Baby and his older brother, Tim, discover that love isn't finite after all: There's plenty of it to go around. You can see the huge amount of love and devotion the artists at Dream-Works have poured into this project by thumbing through the pages of this book. And the results of their hard work are on full display on the big screen. The Boss Baby is packed with memorable characters, insightful revelations, and hilarious jokes. More important, it celebrates human experiences and foibles, and delivers its final message tenderly—with pure, genuine emotion.

I am so thrilled I was asked to be part of this one-of-a-kind experience. I raise a big glass of baby formula to DreamWorks founder and big boss baby Jeffrey Katzenberg, Tom McGrath, Ramsey Naito, Michael McCullers, and all the talented and clever people who brought this beautiful movie to animated life. I think Boss Baby (that's me) is going to give them all a raise this year.

opposite Andy Schuhler; *top* Joe Moshier
following page Alex Puvilland; *pages 10–11* Ritchie Sacilioc

Introduction
Conceiving a Most Unusual Baby

"From the moment the baby arrived. it was obvious that he was the boss."
—*THE BOSS BABY* **BY MARLA FRAZEE**

It's not unusual for children to be concerned about the arrival of a new baby brother or sister in the household. After all, nobody wants to share the love of their parents with a mysterious little person. But what if the new sibling happens to be a strange little character who wears a business suit onesie, carries a briefcase, speaks like a tough-as-nails businessman—in the voice of Alec Baldwin, nonetheless—and has a hidden agenda of his own?

That is the delightful premise of DreamWorks Animation's thirty-fourth movie, *The Boss Baby.* Inspired by the best-selling book of the same name by Marla Frazee, the film takes audiences on a young boy's colorful adventures as he discovers that his new baby brother is not what he seems.

opposite Ritchie Sacilioc; *this page* Joe Moshier

Director Tom McGrath, who is best known for helming DreamWorks' three *Madagascar* blockbusters and its 2010 supervillain fantasy *Megamind*, remembers how the book stood out for him: "I was just finishing *Megamind*, and the development team asked me to look at this stack of books to see if anything piqued my interest," he notes. "There were tons of books about zombies and monsters, and Marla's book really grabbed my attention. It was a charming picture book, just a little over thirty pages long. I pitched to Bill Damaschke (then chief creative officer of DreamWorks) a story told through the point of view of an older brother with a wild imagination."

Damon Ross on the DreamWorks development team was on the same wavelength in thinking this would be a great sibling rivalry story and had started developing the idea with Michael McCullers. Damon connected McGrath and McCullers to flesh out the story, and it ended up being a complementary partnership. Not only had McCullers written and directed the Tina Fey–starring comedy *Baby Mama*, but he also had four kids. He was clearly someone who knew his way around babies.

Finding a way to tell the sibling-rivalry story from the point of view of a distressed and imaginative seven-year-old was their first order of business. "That's the emotional core of the story," McCullers explains. "We realized that there haven't been many children's movies that have addressed the feelings that come with getting a new brother or sister. It's really one of the first elemental family dynamics. It's about sharing love and getting over the jealousy that inevitably comes about."

Since McGrath was the Boss Baby in his family, he also envisioned the story as a love letter to his older brother. "We were immediately struck by the central metaphor of the book—which is what happens when a baby arrives and takes over your house," he says. McCullers adds, "Tom, Damon, and I worked together to come up with ways to explore the origins of this Boss Baby. What kind of a company does he work for? It gave us the chance to explore the birth myth in a terrific and fun way."

The heartfelt nature of the story and the remarkable charm of the main characters were also immediately appealing to producer Ramsey Naito. "The story mirrored my life. My oldest son was seven years old when my youngest arrived, and he was really jealous, just like our main character, Tim. I related to the brother's story instantly," says Naito, whose many credits include *The SpongeBob SquarePants Movie, Jimmy Neutron: Boy Genius, South Park: Bigger, Longer & Uncut*, and the *Rugrats* movie. "I love that we celebrate the power of children's fantasy and imagination in this film."

opposite Joe Moshier; *this page* Alex Puvilland

A Tip of the Hat to Classic Toons

A wonderful story deserves to be told with the right visual style, and the artists at Dream-Works Animation have always been astute about finding the perfect aesthetic to tell each movie's unique tale. For *The Boss Baby*, McGrath and his team were keen on creating a world that looked different from more photorealistic CG films and was a throwback to the elastic, cartoony world of 2-D *Looney Tunes* classics.

"I grew up with those Chuck Jones and Bob Clampett classics," recalls McGrath. "This film gave me the opportunity to do what 2-D was able to do. We wanted these characters to be flexible and fleshy, reminiscent of how Jones and Clampett drew their characters—that world was quite different from the hard, graphic 2-D we see today on TV. A short like Clampett's *The Wise-Quacking Duck*, for example, is one of my all-time favorites: It's really dimensional, but the animation is really broad and snappy."

HE'S WALKING HONEY!

"I grew up with those Chuck Jones and Bob Clampett classics. This film gave me the opportunity to do what 2-D was able to do."

—TOM MCGRATH, DIRECTOR

opposite Joe Moshier; *top* Geefwee Boedoe; *above* Stevie Lewis; *following pages* Max Boas, Chris Brock, Goro Fujita, Ruben Perez, Alex Puvilland, Stevie Lewis, Andy Schuhler, Fred Stewart & Raymond Zibach

Tools of the Future, Eyes on the Past

David James, the film's production designer, points out that it was important for the creative team to pay homage to some of the classic animated shorts and features they all loved and revered. "We are all fans of Chuck Jones and Maurice Noble, and admire the handmade aesthetic of many of the shorts from that golden era of animation," says James. "There was this wonderful sense of nostalgia and charm in Disney's *Lady and the Tramp*, for example, which harkened back to a Victorian-era aesthetic. We wanted to do the same thing but set our movie in a more recent past."

James, a DreamWorks veteran whose numerous credits include *Flushed Away, Monsters vs. Aliens, Megamind,* and *Mr. Peabody & Sherman*, says that, in McGrath's imagination, the movie was always a period piece, but the exact decade had not yet been defined. He explains: "When we actually delved into the nitty gritty of designing the movie, we realized that it absolutely had to be set in a period that we had distant memories of. It is less important when it is than when it's not. It's definitely not now. We borrowed iconic toys, clothes, and objects from many different times, but parents of a certain age may recognize some objects. So, if we've done our jobs right, people are going to see certain toys and say, 'Oh, I remember that!'"

Visual development and lighting consultant Raymond Zibach added, "I was lucky enough to come on to this film during the juicy part. Four or five sequences were well underway in lighting, and you could really see the potential. I feel that the way Tom is using all these references from the golden age of animation that we grew up with will resonate with the audience, young and old. CG animation has tried before but has never been so successful. It's a celebration of why we wanted to be artists in this medium."

The film is also dotted with details taken from the personal family experiences of the studio's

opposite Stevie Lewis; *above* Alex Puvilland

artists. "When Tom pitched me the idea for the movie, I was excited by the fact that the story is driven by a character who is having an experience that is almost universal—the great injustice of siblinghood!" says James. "I am a father of two kids myself, so we had a lot of meetings where we all shared some of the funny truths of domestic existence—both current and remembered. As a designer, it's very exciting to work with this bigger picture. You can ascribe meaning to all the designs when you know where it all needs to go."

Art director Ruben Perez (*Mr. Peabody & Sherman, Madagascar: Escape 2 Africa*) says he was delighted that the film seeks to pay homage to some of his favorite childhood cartoons. "It was a completely different style from the other movies I had worked on before," he points out. "In a way, the goal was to make the CG look like a 2-D film if you squint your eyes. We also had to research the color and the vibrancy so that they wouldn't be a distraction and that they'd match the storytelling style."

To deliver the desired look, Perez and his team created backgrounds with less information, abbreviating the small details to give the characters maximum readability. The backgrounds then became loose impressions that left some room for the audience to interpret and fill in the blanks. "We also used gobo shapes, or spotlight shapes, to frame characters and maximize the focus," explains Perez. "The color throughout the film, and especially when experiencing an event through Tim's imagination, has a vibrant, inviting quality. The sun seems to reach every corner of this universe!"

right Stevie Lewis

Powered by Imagination

Head of story Ennio Torresan also connected immediately with the poignant human emotions evoked by key sequences in the movie. "I worked with Tom on *Megamind* and the *Madagascar* movies, and we share the same sense of humor," he says. "The fact that we also go in and out of the mind of our main character, Tim, was something that we had never done before, and I loved it. I have two young kids myself, so I was also dealing with sibling jealousy issues at home. Every Monday, I would tell Tom stories about what happened at home and how my kids almost killed me over the weekend, so we tried to use our own experiences in the movie as well!"

Torresan, who draws storyboards using pencil, paper, and Photoshop, found a lot of inspiration in the works of legendary animators Friz Freleng and Tex Avery. "Freleng was such a great model for the timing of music and scores," he notes. "I love to watch his movies and really observe how he was able to create such masterpieces. Avery's surreal humor was also a big influence. I like to think of our director Tom as crazy, brilliant, and comedic like Mozart. He breathes comedy, and we all try to emulate him."

This reverence for a retro 2-D animation style and the desire to create memorable and loveable characters are also dear to Carlos Puertolas, the movie's head of animation. A DreamWorks veteran whose credits include *Madagascar: Escape 2 Africa*, *Madagascar 3*, *Rise of the Guardians*, and

Home, Puertolas says he knew the movie was going to be special the minute he heard McGrath's pitch. "It's the perfect movie to be animated because it's told from the perspective of a little kid," he says. "Imagination plays a big role in children's lives, as it does in our movie."

Puertolas and the rest of the animation team worked hard to makes sure the characters looked appealing from every angle. "Take Boss Baby, for example: We are hearing Alec Baldwin's voice, but the character is a cute, charming baby," Puertolas notes. "You want the audience to want to grab his cheeks. It's the same thing with Tim. You want him to be a likable seven-year-old boy. What may seem charming to an adult may seem wimpy to a young moviegoer. You don't want Tim to be a crybaby, but he needs to have a little bit of an attitude to resonate with younger audiences."

opposite Andy Schuhler; *above* Geefwee Boedoe

Style and Substance

For head of layout Kent Seki, the film provided a chance to experiment with different cinematographic styles, especially during Tim's fantasy sequences. "We were able to push the stereoscopic elements of those sequences because Tim is having these elaborate adventures in his imagination," says Seki. "We were also able to explore tilt-shift–style photography—something that we hadn't done before. This style of photography moves the camera plane and rotates the lens, creating a more intimate, miniature effect. It makes the characters feel small and vulnerable at Baby Corp. After Boss Baby leaves the corporation to return to his family, we turn the effect off to make the stereo and the focus become deeper. It reinforces the emotional content of the moment."

Another aspect of the film that makes it unique is the way McGrath uses dynamic action and extensive previsualization work to map out the cinematography. "We were constantly trying to improve the performances, especially how the characters emote," Seki says. "We re-examined the character rigs to get the best character emotion possible. We were constantly reviewing the lighting with the art designers and got a better blueprint in the process. Overall, I have to say that we have come up with a film that embraces the heritage of animation through both its aesthetic and storytelling choices. It really shows off the medium."

One of the main challenges for the film's lead editor, Jim Ryan, was finding the right moments and coming up with the best way to approach them. "The animation style of the movie—particularly the comedy bits—is very broad," he explains. "We can be broader with the comedy, cut things a little tighter, and take a more cartoony approach with those moments."

Ryan's fondness for classic action-adventure films helped shape Tim's imaginary sequences. "Tim goes into four different fantasies—he's running in a jungle, gets into a brawl with a gorilla, mans a spaceship, and drives under the sea to rescue his parents from sharks, so we used the editing style to be reminiscent of some of those familiar movies."

opposite top Ruben Perez & Andy Schuhler; *opposite bottom* Andy Schuhler
above Raymond Zibach and Andy Schuhler

Feats of Visual Magic

So if you are producing an animated movie about a typical suburban family and their unusual baby, what kinds of CG visual effects will come in handy? As it turns out, delivering the goods for this family tale was just as—if not more—challenging as preparing a big summer tentpole picture.

"Working on all the details in Tim's room with all the toys can be just as complex as creating an imaginary chase in the backyard where we need to

come up with fun effects for the grass," says senior visual effects supervisor Ken Bielenberg, a veteran of the *Shrek* films, *Puss in Boots*, and *Monsters vs. Aliens*. "There is so much action in that chase scene that we had to make sure all the characters are going to read clearly even though they're moving quickly. We also had to figure out how to go from CG characters, environments, and trees back to the more stylized and painterly matte paintings gracefully."

Bielenberg mentions that although *The Boss Baby* is not an "effects" film, per se, it showcases plenty of sequences that demanded clever use of technology. A good example is a scene in which Boss Baby is pretending to be sick to distract his babysitter, Eugene. "This extended sequence of projectile vomit had to be planned out in detail," says Bielenberg. "The liquid interacts with the characters—the hair and clothes—and it affects all the surfacing work. You need a history of where exactly all the vomit has gone and interacted with the material."

Senior visual effects supervisor Tony K. Williams says McGrath's love for the classic era of animation and artists such as Mary Blair has made a huge impact on how the team is incorporating the 2-D style into their designs and visuals. "It's not easy to make something look simple," he says. "Our job is to distill shapes down to the absolute minimum. In some of the other movies I've worked on, we just had to add more details, and it's easier that way. Our job here is to get clean, crisp animation. You just can't hide anything!"

To make Boss Baby's face look as appealing as possible, Williams and his team had to work with extreme geometrical deformations. "We had to make these shapes conform to a particular aesthetic—with these very large eyes and appealing facial expressions," he explains. "Another highlight is the hair we were able to create in this film. I'm very proud of Tim's hair—it's been crafted to look great at every possible angle!"

Working on all the babies as they move on the conveyer belt in Baby Corp. was one of visual effects supervisor Vanitha Rangaraju's favorite parts of the assignment. "It's a dreamlike sequence during which we introduce Boss Baby," she says. "We wanted this ethereal, heavenly quality. Our goal was to see the hand of the artist coming through beyond the CG technology and to directly connect with the audience."

Rangaraju says that, in some instances, the crowd department had to produce close to four hundred babies for one scene. "Of course, we had done crowds for many of our movies before, but they didn't compare to this one. The babies' skin had to feel translucent and soft. Our texture department had to work very hard to achieve that quality. We used lots of subsurface scattering—a mechanism of light transport in which light penetrates the surface of a translucent object—to let the light through the skin."

opposite Ruben Perez; *right* Andy Gaskill

A Tale of Two Continents

Since most of the film's surfacing, modeling, visual effects, matte painting, crowds, and lighting work were done by the DreamWorks Dedicated Unit in Bangalore, India, the studio's Glendale, California–based artists had to communicate around the clock to make up for the twelve- to thirteen-hour time difference between the two regions. A more compressed production schedule also added more challenges for the two teams.

"Our director [Tom McGrath] worked very closely with our team in India from launch to final output," says Bangalore-based digital supervisor Vimal Subramaniam. "He has inspired the whole crew in DDU and made it feel like it's our own movie."

"It's not easy to make something look simple. Our job is to distill shapes down to the absolute minimum. You just can't hide anything!"

—TONY K. WILLIAMS, SENIOR VISUAL EFFECTS SUPERVISOR

Subramaniam says the film feels and looks very different from other projects he has worked on previously: "Unlike other movies, we directed the look to match the mood of our protagonist, Tim. When he thinks he is the center of the world, he is in light, and when he thinks he's not, he's out of light. The color palette has a mix of analogous and complementary color schemes, all based on the mood of the film. Also, our lighting is very character-centric and art directed to express Tim's emotions all the time. The matte painting is very impressionistic, and the surfacing is stylized—that even includes the wood patterns on the furniture!"

Effects supervisor Mitul Patel adds, "All the other films we have worked on have had very realistic shapes and timing, but for *Boss Baby*, the effects are used to make the film funnier. The shapes are simple, but they're art directed, and the timing is very snappy and cartoony. This was challenging at the time, because our tools (i.e. solvers) are built on real-world physics, so we had to work a little harder to achieve the film's desired look and timings."

Lighting supervisor Rajarajan Ramakrishnan, who also works at the DreamWorks Dedicated Unit in Bangalore, says McGrath was very particular about one simple thing: the "light is love" philosophy. "We needed to understand this simple philosophy and use our tools and techniques to fulfill his vision," he says. "I'm a father of a two-year-old girl, and because the film deals with the emotional bond between siblings, it meant a lot to me. We were dealing with a very intimate space visually. The choices of our light setups and optical nuances had to reflect all of the film's special performances and heartfelt emotions."

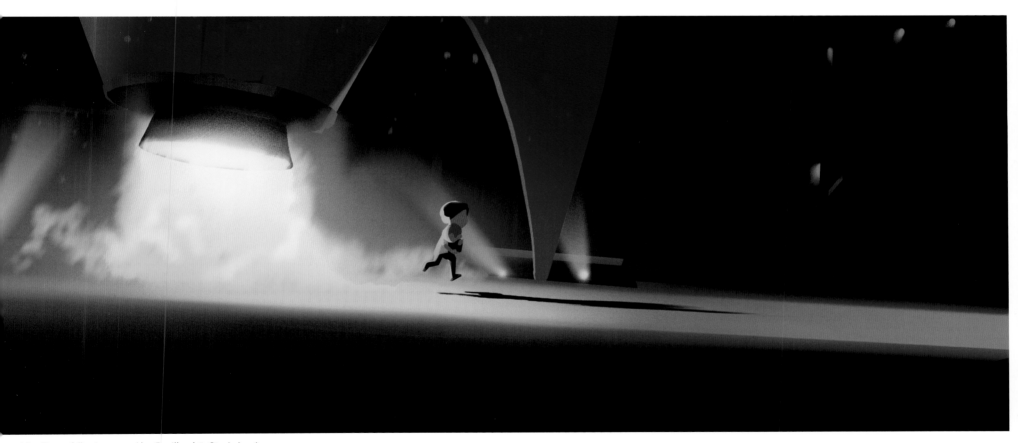

Boss Baby

There was a lot riding on the design of the central character of the movie. Boss Baby had to be as cute and lovable as could be, but he also needed to be a believable vessel for Alec Baldwin's savvy businessman voice.

"The movie is an intimate character story with Boss Baby and Tim," says director Tom McGrath. "Therefore we needed the characters to have appeal and charm, and we were fortunate to have

Joe Moshier (*Mr. Peabody & Sherman, Penguins of Madagascar*) design him in 2-D, as if we were doing the movie in 2-D. The goal was to find the charm, the shape language, the proportions of the eyes, and the kind of expressions that we loved, and then see how we could convert that into a 3-D character."

The design team played with a delicate balance as they created a beautiful baby who could

above, far right, opposite top left, opposite top right, opposite center, opposite bottom center, and *opposite bottom right* Joe Moshier; *opposite center left, opposite center right,* and *opposite bottom left* Tom McGrath

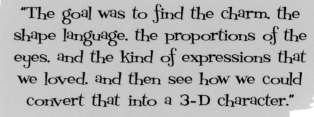

SUPERSEDED

also push everyone around and demand authority. "Boss Baby is the representation of the nebulous idea of this businessman," says production designer David James. "This is Alec Baldwin, after all."

Producer Ramsey Naito adds, "Alec Baldwin is the soul of this character. There is no Boss Baby without Alec."

To get all the facial expressions right, the animators studied hours of videos of babies on the Internet. What proved quite useful, according to the director, were videos that captured babies' first reactions to experiences such as hearing music, tasting something sour or sweet, or encountering a family pet.

As head of animation Carlos Puertolas points out, "Our baby is a real charmer. He is totally playing to the parents. He plays the cutest baby in the world, and even when he is alone with Tim, he retains his charming qualities. He still needs his baby formula and regular naps!"

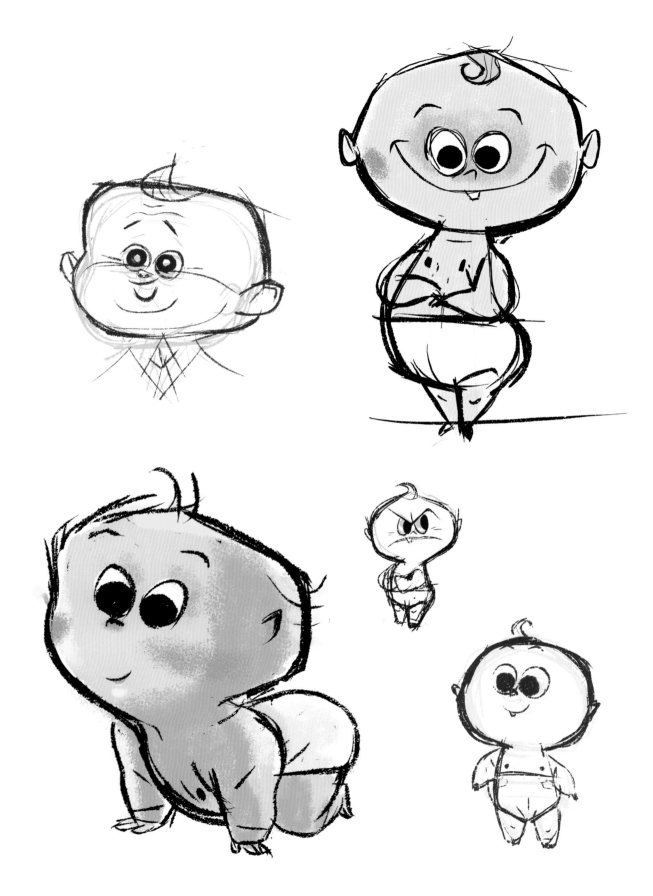

"Our baby is a real charmer. He plays the cutest baby in the world. and even when he is alone with Tim. he retains his charming qualities."

—CARLOS PUERTOLAS, HEAD OF ANIMATION

opposite, top center, top right, center left, center right, and above Joe Moshier; *far left* Andy Schuhler

"Boss Baby is the representation of the nebulous idea of this businessman."
—DAVID JAMES,
PRODUCTION DESIGNER

left Andy Schuhler
top center, top right, above, right, and opposite Joe Moshier

"My brother was only two years older than me. but he was Tim. He was my best friend. and I loved him very much. but there was a time when we were very antagonistic and competitive."

—TOM MCGRATH, DIRECTOR

Tim

Tim, the imaginative young boy whose life is turned upside down by the arrival of Boss Baby, is the sturdy anchor of the movie. Tim is also the film's unreliable narrator through whom the audience experiences the entire story.

"I was the youngest in my family—so I was basically Boss Baby," says director Tom McGrath. "My brother was only two years older than me, but he was Tim. He was my best friend, and I loved him very much, but there was a time when we were very antagonistic and competitive."

Tim's character design was inspired by early sketches by artist Andy Schuhler (*Megamind, Penguins of Madagascar*). "There was one drawing that really captured the character," recalls production designer David James. "Here was this slightly disorganized kid in oversized clothes. He's not exactly cool, and he still has stars in his eyes. He's a happy

opposite Stevie Lewis *&* Joe Moshier; *top, far left, and above* Joe Moshier

top left, top center, top right, center, left, right, and opposite Joe Moshier; *far right* Andy Schuhler

"He's a happy and dreamy guy. His clothes are wrinkled, and his hair is just a little bit messy. He is a kid with a big imagination."

—DAVID JAMES,
PRODUCTION DESIGNER

and dreamy guy. His clothes are wrinkled, and his hair is just a little bit messy. He is a kid with a big imagination. That really informed his design."

"We wanted Tim to look and feel authentic; the way he speaks and perceives his world had to feel like a real kid because Boss Baby is the adult in the relationship. Their character contrast is what drives the comedic engine of the film," says producer Ramsey Naito. Head of animation Carlos Puertolas points out that a young kid who adults find charming may not seem appealing to the younger audiences of the movie. Tim's animation supervisors, Bryce McGovern and Anthony Hodgson, were very aware of the fact that the character had to be charming to people of all ages. "We wanted him to be the hero. He also had to have a little attitude so that kids could connect with him," says Puertolas.

For head of story Ennio Torresan, it's Tim's dynamic with Boss Baby that really defines him. "They don't want to deal with each other in the beginning, but their journey is what makes me love them so much," he says. "I fall in love with them as they begin to love each other."

Animation fans will be interested to know that Tim is voiced by Miles Bakshi, the son of indie animation legend Ralph Bakshi (*Fritz the Cat*, *The Lord of the Rings*). Miles also voiced the Ogre Baby in DreamWorks' *Shrek Forever After* and *Shrek the Halls* TV special.

Timmy PJ's

A   B   C   D   E   F

> "We wanted him to be the hero. He also had to have a little attitude so that kids could connect with him."
>
> —CARLOS PUERTOLAS, HEAD OF ANIMATION

opposite top, above, and right Joe Moshier; *opposite bottom and following pages* Stevie Lewis; *far right* Andy Schuhler

SAFARI

SCUBA

MUMMY

MUMMY HOME

PJs

NAUTICAL

TYKTWD

ROYAL

SPY

PIRATE

GRAD

GROOM

BIKING
OUTFIT

NINJA

SPACE

SPACE HOME

above left Stevie Lewis & Joe Moshier; *above right* Stevie Lewis; *opposite* Joe Moshier

Tim and Boss Baby as Old Men

Mom and Dad

Voiced by Lisa Kudrow and Jimmy Kimmel, Tim's parents are simply oblivious to the chaos unleashed by Boss Baby in their household. Barely hanging on to the slightest resemblance of domestic order at home, they have no clue about the strange machinations of Baby Corp. and Puppy Co.

"The parents have a new baby in the house and are both working full-time. They are sleep-deprived and barely holding it together, and this needed to be captured in their design," says producer Ramsey Naito. "We wanted to get away from an idealized version of parents," says production designer David James. "Mom, especially, needed to be a very real person with a realistic body. At the same time, she had to exude this warmth. Her beauty and her maternal nature go hand in hand."

Meanwhile, Tim's dad is just trying to keep up. "Like many new fathers, he has this slight deer-in-headlights look," notes James. "He tries his best to keep everything under control, but he is a bit over-whelmed by all the changes. They are both loving parents—and the lesson of the movie is that there is love enough going around for everybody. They do have unconditional love for both of their kids, and that's something that Tim learns by the end of the movie. Because the movie is told through Tim's point of view, the parents seem like the desired ideal. But we, the audience, can see their humanity and imperfections, and that's something we tried to celebrate in the design as well."

these pages Joe Moshier

above, top right, and opposite page Joe Moshier
right Andy Schuhler

"Mom, especially, needed to be a very real person with a realistic body. At the same time, she had to exude this warmth. Her beauty and her maternal nature go hand in hand."

—DAVID JAMES, PRODUCTION DESIGNER

these pages Joe Moshier

Boss Baby's Special Mission Team

Every boss needs a group of harried underlings who are always running around trying to execute all of his orders. That's why the creative team brought the Triplets, Staci, and Jimbo into the picture. Initially, the plan was to have adult actors voice the babies, but they quickly realized that it would be much more frustrating for Boss Baby if his special task force acted and sounded like a bunch of toddlers.

"We designed them to be as adorable and charming as they could be," says director Tom McGrath. "We wanted them to be fun and really great to spend time with. They are the comic relief of the movie. We also wanted to celebrate diversity by showcasing these multicultural characters."

The team is used heavily in two impossible chase scenes. Acting as a special mission team, they chase Tim around in the backyard in order to retrieve an incriminating tape of Boss Baby. "Each one of them has a specialty," says production designer David James. "When they work together, they become like a superhero team. It's the whole Voltron idea of the collective over the individual!"

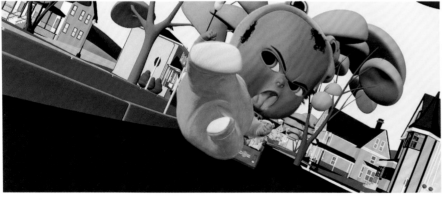

opposite Stevie Lewis

The Triplets

The triplets behave like "yes-men" and agree with whatever Boss Baby says. "They're brilliant, kinetic, and unflappably optimistic—and they are very cute running around in their frog, cat, and duck onesies," says director Tom McGrath. "They are also very good at martial arts and performing acrobatic stunts!"

"We designed them to be as adorable and charming as they could be. They are the comic relief of the movie."

—TOM MCGRATH, DIRECTOR

these pages Stevie Lewis

these pages Stevie Lewis

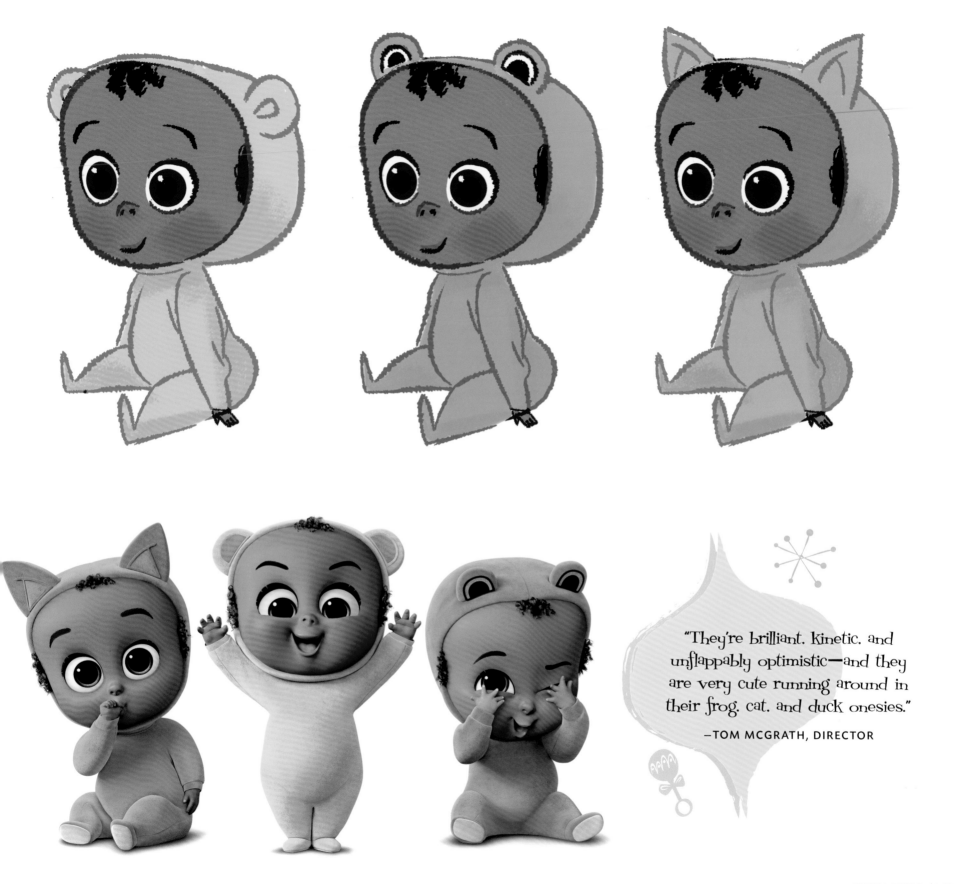

"They're brilliant, kinetic, and unflappably optimistic—and they are very cute running around in their frog, cat, and duck onesies."

—TOM MCGRATH, DIRECTOR

these pages Stevie Lewis

Staci

Staci is the eager intern of the group, ready to take her next assignment. "She acts as a court stenographer, but her notes leave a lot to be desired," joke producer Ramsey Naito and director Tom McGrath. "She is also a super-adorable over-achiever, just like me," beams Naito.

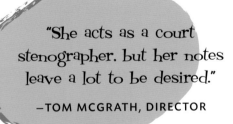

"She acts as a court stenographer, but her notes leave a lot to be desired."

—TOM MCGRATH, DIRECTOR

these pages Stevie Lewis

Jimbo

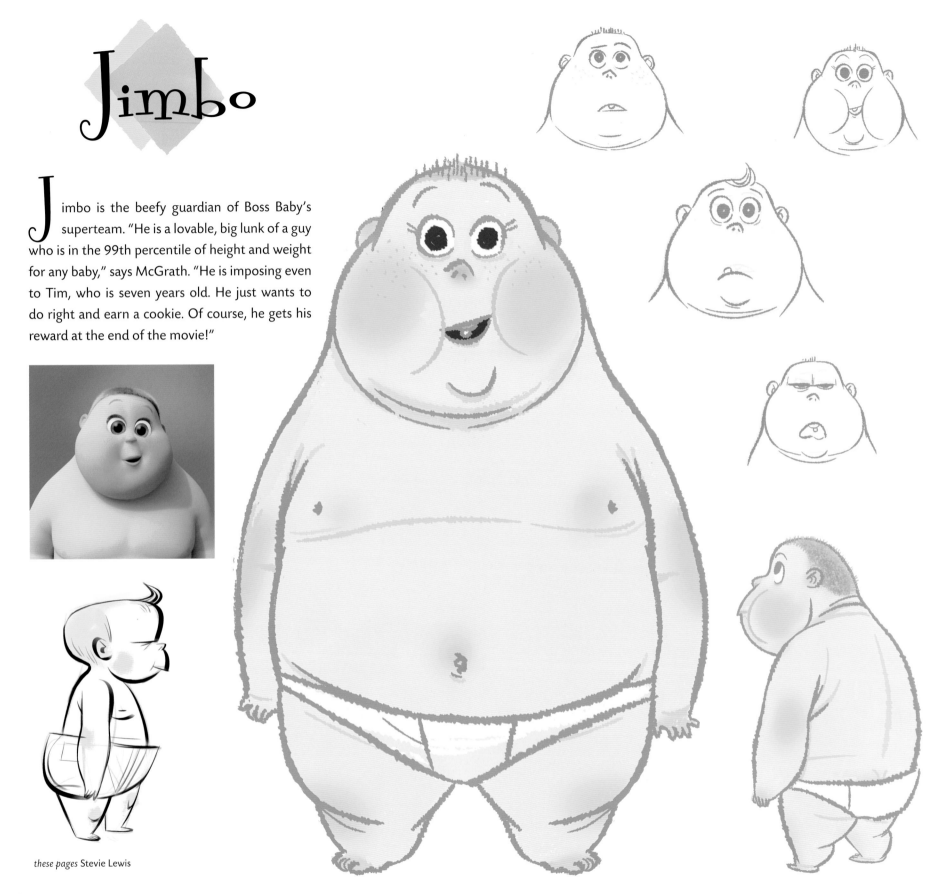

Jimbo is the beefy guardian of Boss Baby's superteam. "He is a lovable, big lunk of a guy who is in the 99th percentile of height and weight for any baby," says McGrath. "He is imposing even to Tim, who is seven years old. He just wants to do right and earn a cookie. Of course, he gets his reward at the end of the movie!"

these pages Stevie Lewis

"He is a lovable, big lunk of a guy who is in the 99th percentile of height and weight for any baby. He just wants to do right and earn a cookie."

—TOM MCGRATH, DIRECTOR

Lamb Lamb

Like many of the toys and fixtures seen in the movie, Tim's cherished stuffed lamb was inspired by a real-life family experience. The addition of Lamb Lamb was the result of a photo of a similar toy brought in by writer Michael McCullers. "His daughter owned a lamb plush that she really loved, and we thought it would be great to draw this from reality," says director Tom McGrath.

The artists put their own spin on the lamb plush. The toy plays an important role in a tough hostage situation and gets torn apart as a result of the conflict between Boss Baby and Tim. "Tim's Voltron toy represents a new toy, and Lamb Lamb was one of those older classic toys. Boss Baby fixes it and gives it back to Tim when they say good-bye, and that is seen as a sweet gesture on his part," says McGrath. "It's woven into the story quite nicely."

this page and opposite right Stevie Lewis; *opposite left* Tom McGrath

WiZZie

Tim's cherished wizard alarm clock was inspired by an early background drawing by artist Radford Sechrist (*Penguins of Madagascar, How to Train Your Dragon 2*).

"We loved the idea that this wizard-shaped alarm clock is Tim's one and only friend," explains McGrath. "They have some great moments together. Sechrist's sketch is a perfect example of how a great drawing can inspire a whole character. We boarded this scene in which Tim talks to his alarm clock to get inspiration from him, and it worked very well. We also had a lot of fun with Wizzie throughout the movie, exploring the whole point of view of being a clock and how he gets confused by daylight savings!"

CROOK AT END

MOON STARS ON HAT ONLY?

SWIVEL AT SASH

MOLDED PLASTIC DRAPERY

MUSHROOM SNOOZE BUTTON

PLASTIC STUMP

Big Boss Baby

Big Boss Baby is Boss Baby's direct supervisor. She was definitely designed to look like a very imposing character. In the movie, we learn that she deposed Francis Francis as the head of Baby Corp., and that she was the original mastermind behind the company's very successful Baby Boom. "She certainly stands out from all the other babies," says production designer David James. "Her fun, exaggerated design came directly from the mind of Joe Moshier *(Mr. Peabody & Sherman, Penguins of Madagascar)*. I love the fact that she has more hair than all the other babies in the movie!"

these pages Joe Moshier

"She certainly stands out from all the other babies. Her fun, exaggerated design came directly from the mind of Joe Moshier."

—DAVID JAMES, PRODUCTION DESIGNER

these pages Joe Moshier

left Andy Schuhler; *top, above, opposite center, and opposite right* Joe Moshier; *opposite left* Andy Schuhler

Francis Francis

Voiced by Steve Buscemi, Francis E. Francis is the CEO of Puppy Co. and is described as an angry, bitter, and lonely character. His character went through the most change throughout the development of the movie. "We started off with the idea that he is a larger-than-life guy who seems joyful, like a manager at a friendly neighborhood grocery store," says director Tom McGrath. "But then we realized that he has this dark, sinister plan, and it would be interesting to explore this duality."

However, since the film had to be told through the adult Tim's point of view, it would be difficult to deal with this revelation about Francis. "It's a movie about a kid who has grown up and is reflecting about how his brother came into his life," explains McGrath. "It's not the kind of movie where you can switch over to the villain and see him planning and scheming. So the big idea was that he was this revered, supercolossal, big, bad, giant Boss Baby in Baby Corp., but nobody really knew what had happened to him. What really happened was that he got fired and then grew bitter, and he ended up becoming this savvy businessman. We even figured that he invented the Baby Boom and put Baby Corp. on the map!"

"He is the imagined villain," offers production designer David James. "He is an embodiment of Tim's desire to be an only child. He symbolizes a life lived without the love of a sibling. He even appeals to Tim, telling him that he knows how he feels. He is Tim grown old without a brother—not so much in his design but in the nature of his character."

"We started off with the idea that he is a larger-than-life guy who seems joyful. But then we realized that he has this dark, sinister plan, and it would be interesting to explore this duality."

—TOM MCGRATH, DIRECTOR

opposite and above Joe Moshier; *right* Andy Schuhler

opposite Andy Schuhler; *this page* Joe Moshier

Eugene

Francis Francis's brother can be described as a monosyllabic brute, but he is also seen as a path to redemption for Francis Francis. "He turns out to be a force of love," says production designer David James. "All brothers are redeemed in this film, despite their seemingly broken relationships."

The designs of Francis Francis and Eugene are worlds apart. Although they are siblings, they are profoundly different in terms of their outward appearances.

these pages Joe Moshier

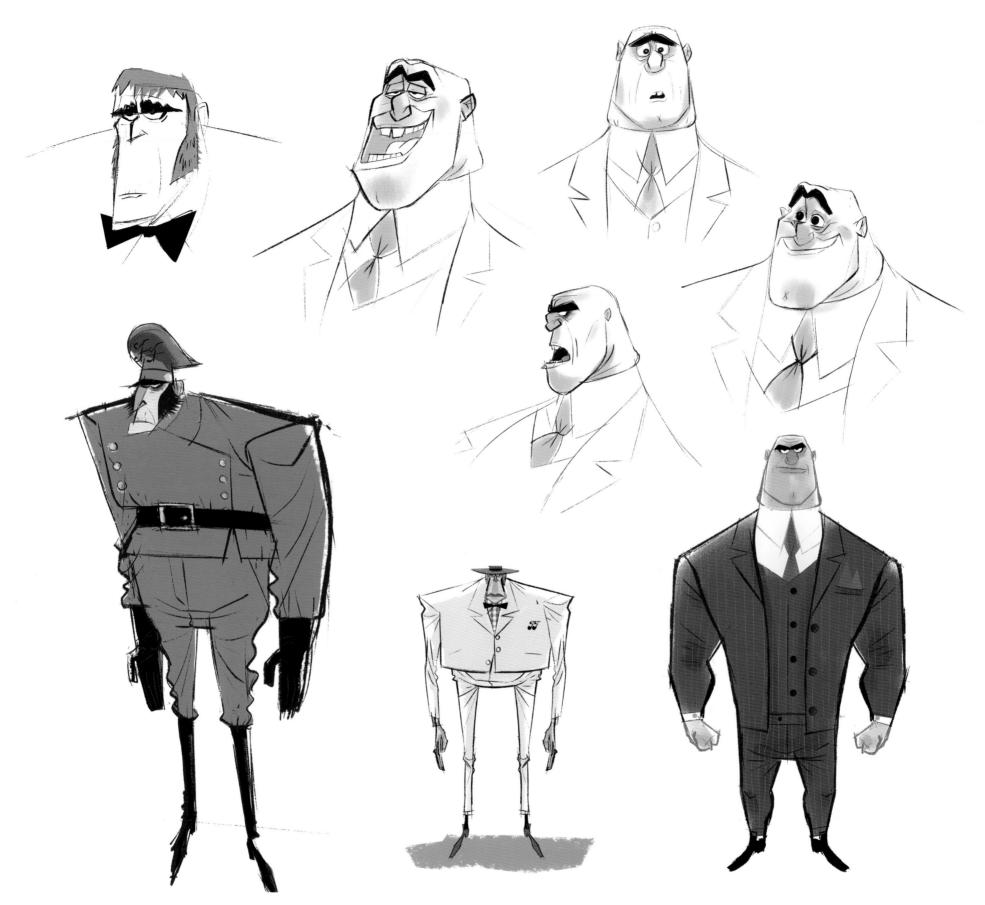

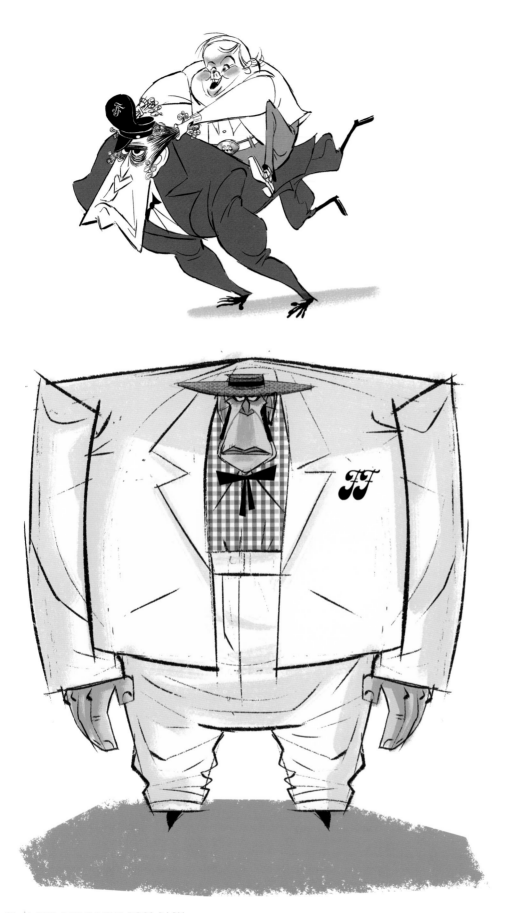

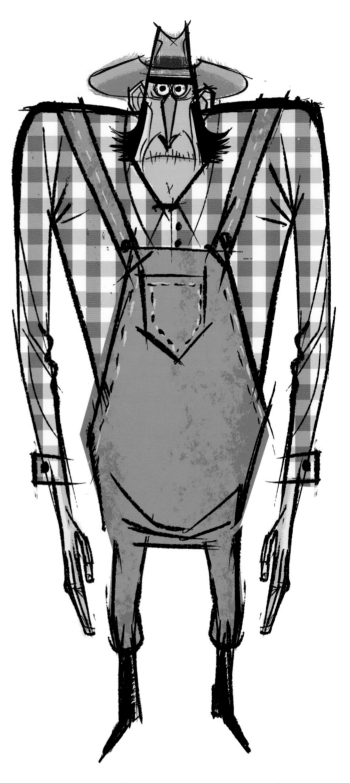

top left Andy Schuhler; *left, above, and opposite* Joe Moshier

Forever Puppy

How do you come up with the world's most adorable puppy, created to steal hearts and capture all the love in human households? You study lots and lots of cute videos of puppies on the Internet. That's part of what the design team did to come up with the ultimate design for Forever Puppy. They also enjoyed visits from live puppies—courtesy of animator Dan Wagner and his rescue animals. "Forever Puppy is the impossibly saccharine version of puppyhood who can potentially threaten the existence of humanity," says production designer David James. Just think of it as a cuddly fluff ball with giant eyes.

opposite Andy Schuhler; *this page* Joe Moshier

previous page and *these pages* Joe Moshier; *following pages* Stevie Lewis

Tim's House

The house in which Tim and his parents live peacefully before the arrival of Boss Baby was designed to have fantastic dimensions to echo how the world seems to a seven-year-old boy. "In this universe, we had to allow for whimsy and charm but also for the slight impossibility of what is going on—by making this world slightly more fantastic than a regular home," says director Tom McGrath.

That's why the house seems larger in its dimensionality and verticality than actual house measurements. "The shapes are definitely pushed, and the world seems quite stylized," says production designer David James. "It's similar to this idea that when you return to your parents' house as an adult, you have this bizarre moment of scale disconnect. You say to yourself, 'Wow, I remember this, but it seemed so much bigger when I was a kid.' That's what we were going for."

The house also goes through a monumental change when the baby arrives. "It changes from this pristine, perfect environment built for Tim into an invasion landscape of laundry and toys left behind," says James. "Anyone who has had a baby has experienced this same chaos!"

"[The house] changes from this pristine, perfect environment built for Tim into an invasion landscape of laundry and toys left behind. Anyone who has had a baby has experienced this same chaos!"

—DAVID JAMES, PRODUCTION DESIGNER

opposite top and following pages Alex Puvilland; *opposite bottom left* Joe Moshier; *opposite center right* Radford Sechrist; *opposite bottom right* Dave Needham; *top* Geefwee Boedoe; *above* David Huang

opposite Frederic Stewart; *this page* Pete Maynez

1

4

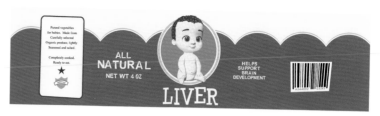

ALL NATURAL
NET WT 4 OZ

HELPS
SUPPORT
BRAIN
DEVELOPMENT

LIVER

ALL NATURAL
NET WT 4 OZ

HELPS
SUPPORT
BRAIN
DEVELOPMENT

VEAL

ALL NATURAL
NET WT 4 OZ

HELPS
SUPPORT
BRAIN
DEVELOPMENT

PEAS

5

WITH SHINE POWER
SHING!
tooth paste
NET WT. 3.8 oz

2

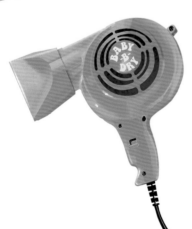

BABY B DRY

3

DAIRY
MILK
VITAMIN A & D

6

MÜSK
BY FREDERIC STEWART

AFTERSHAVE LOTION

7

Poof

Baby
Powder

8

these pages Vy Trinh & Frederic Stewart
following pages Andy Schuhler

opposite and top right Stevie Lewis; *top left* Geefwee Boedoe; *above* Alex Puvilland

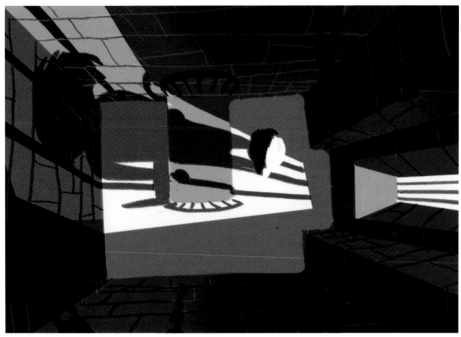

"In this universe. we had to allow for whimsy and charm but also for the slight impossibility of what is going on—by making this world slightly more fantastic than a regular home."

—TOM MCGRATH, DIRECTOR

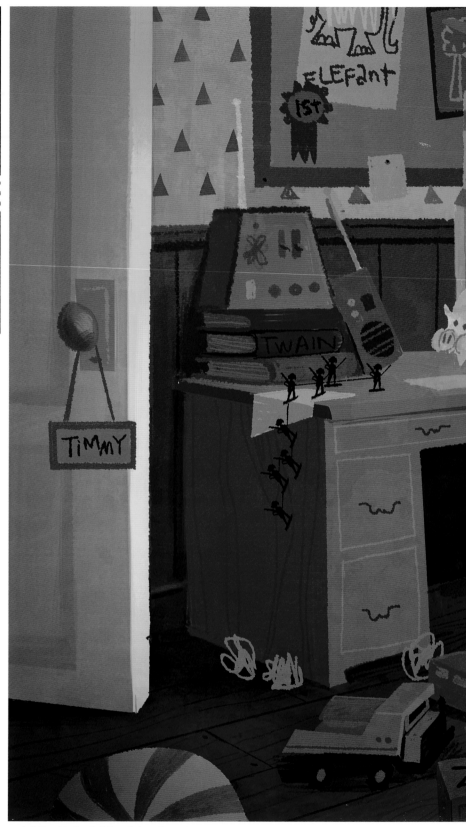

top left Tom McGrath; *left and above* Stevie Lewis

timmy's ROOM

this page and opposite bottom Stevie Lewis; *opposite top left* Frederic Stewart; *opposite top right* Vy Trinh

The Neighborhood

The movie is set in an unspecified year in a not-so-distant past, and that's why Tim's neighborhood also had to be located in an idyllic Spielbergian suburbia. "We knew the film had to be a period piece, and we wanted the neighborhood to look like something you would see in Middle America," notes director Tom McGrath. "We studied architecture and found houses that really reflected that typical Midwestern architecture."

McGrath says they really wanted the neighborhood streets to have curves to them, with plenty of trees and topography. "You usually see simpler grids in animated features, because doing otherwise makes it more expensive," he adds. "But we really wanted it to be supercharming, reminiscent of the 1970s, like something out of *E.T. the Extra-Terrestrial*."

Tim's house was also meant to be a modest curbside charmer. "We didn't want Tim to be this wealthy kid, someone who is entitled," says McGrath. "We wanted him to be from a modest middle-class family with two working parents."

above and opposite center right Alex Puvilland; *opposite top, opposite center left, opposite center, and opposite bottom* Ruben Perez

SILVER
BOOTS

Tim's Fantasies

Some of the most fantastic sequences in the movie take place in Tim's mind as he imagines larger-than-life adventures. Inspired in part by Indiana Jones films and your typical child's imaginary games with their toys, these sequences are more brightly colored than the other parts of the movie. You can think of it as Tim's versions of his favorite comic strips, in which a boy fights aliens in space, swings from vines in jungles, and battles sharks in the depth of the ocean—all thanks to the magic of his active imagination.

opposite top Stevie Lewis; *opposite bottom* Colin Jack
this page Joe Moshier

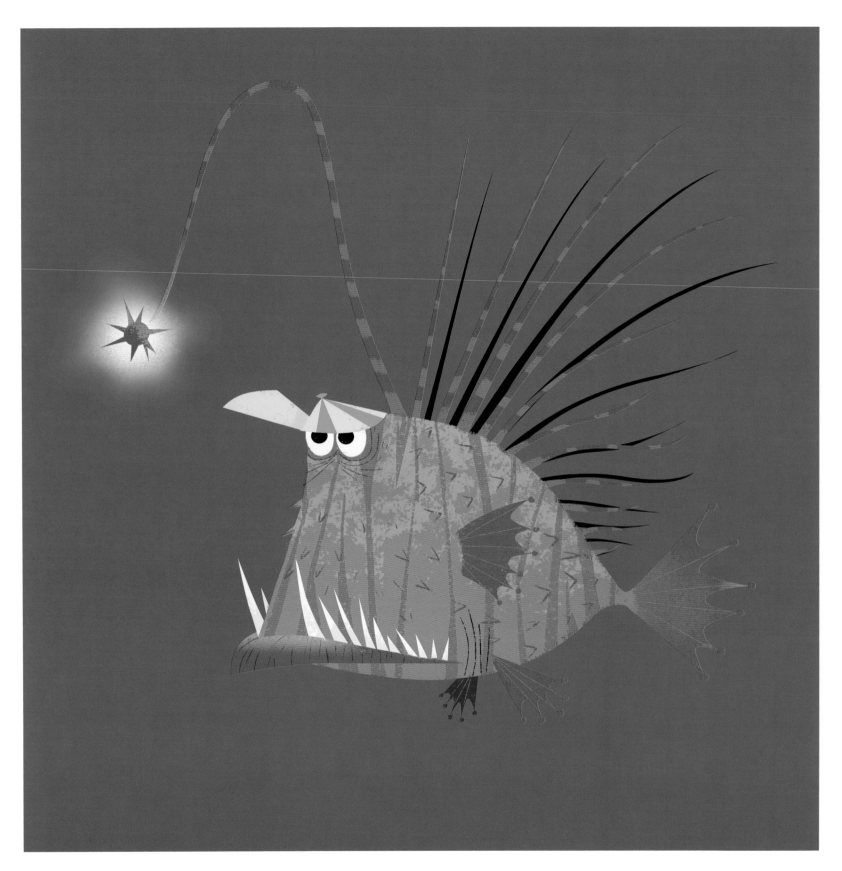

these pages Joe Moshier; *following pages* Ennio Torresan

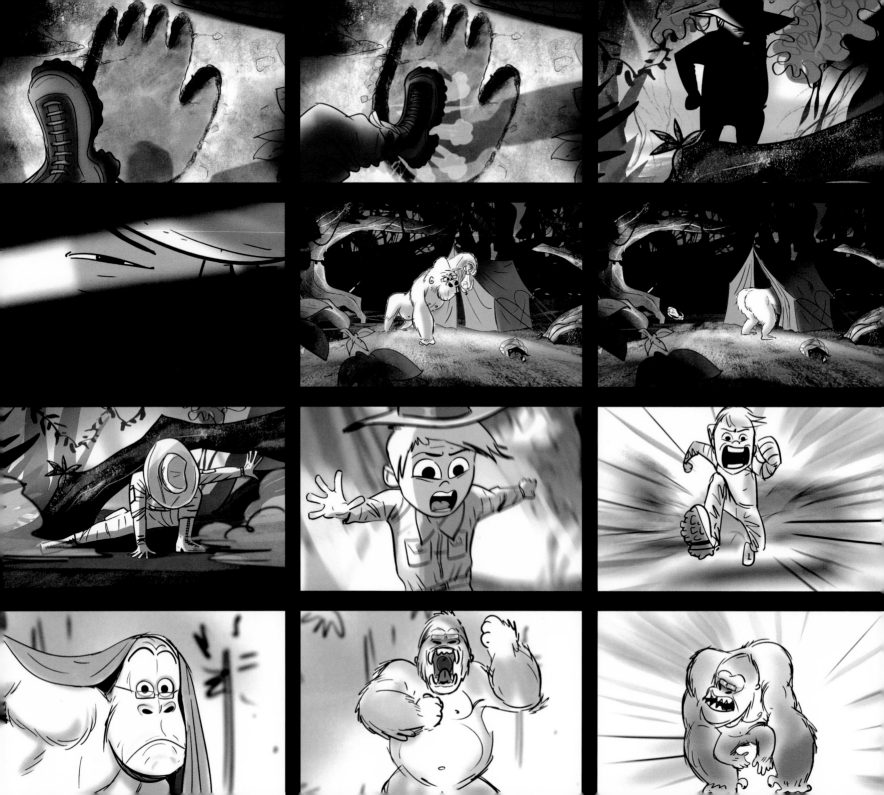

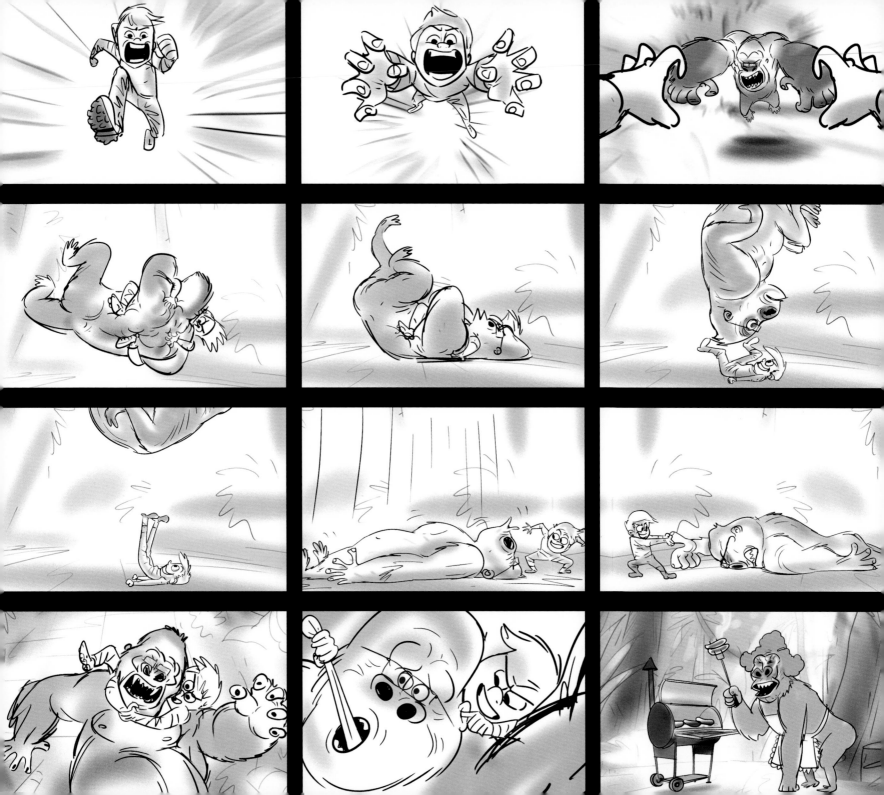

these pages Joe Moshier; *following pages top* Tom McGrath
following pages bottom Colin Jack

Tim's fantasies are his own personal versions of his favorite comic strips. in which a boy fights aliens in space. swings from vines in jungles. and battles sharks in the depth of the ocean—all thanks to the magic of his active imagination.

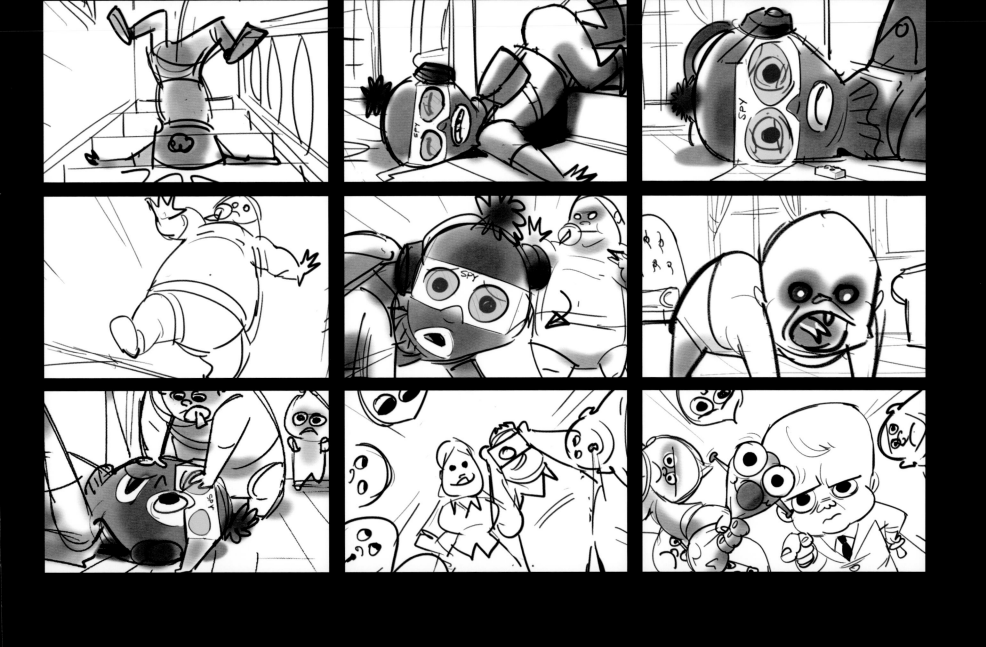

above Stevie Lewis; *opposite* Andy Schuhler; *page 124 top* Ruben Perez
page 124–125 bottom Radford Sechrist; *page 125* Andy Schuhler & Raymond Zibach

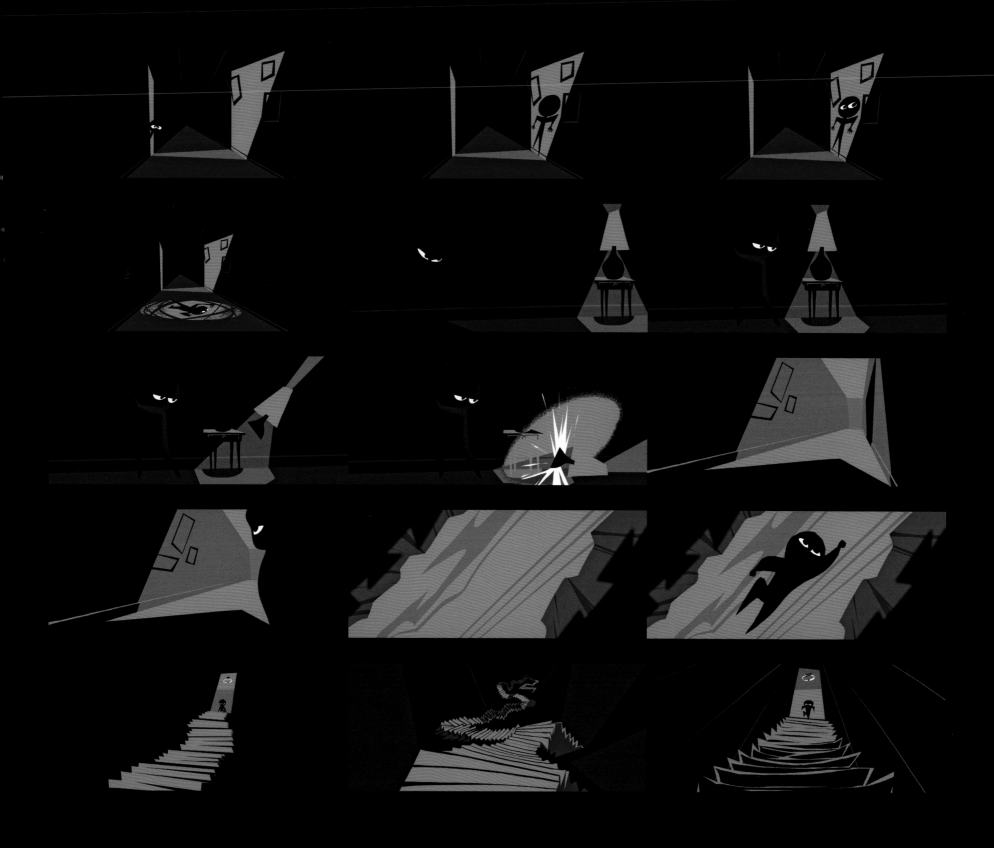

Baby Corp.

The visuals for a heavenly conveyor-belt factory where babies are created and diapered and sent to their families around the world were some of the first images that came to director Tom McGrath's mind as he was watching a documentary series that featured mid-century architecture.

"Baby Corp. reminds me of the height of mid-century corporate existence," says production designer David James. Within its actual design, there's this mesmerizing clockwork machinery. The baby factory has all the beautiful motions of one of those incredible assembly lines, but at the same time, it exudes this ethereal lightness."

these pages Alex Puvilland

these pages and following pages Alex Puvilland

Babycorp Interior

"The baby factory has all the beautiful motions of one of those incredible assembly lines. but at the same time it exudes this ethereal lightness."

—DAVID JAMES, PRODUCTION DESIGNER

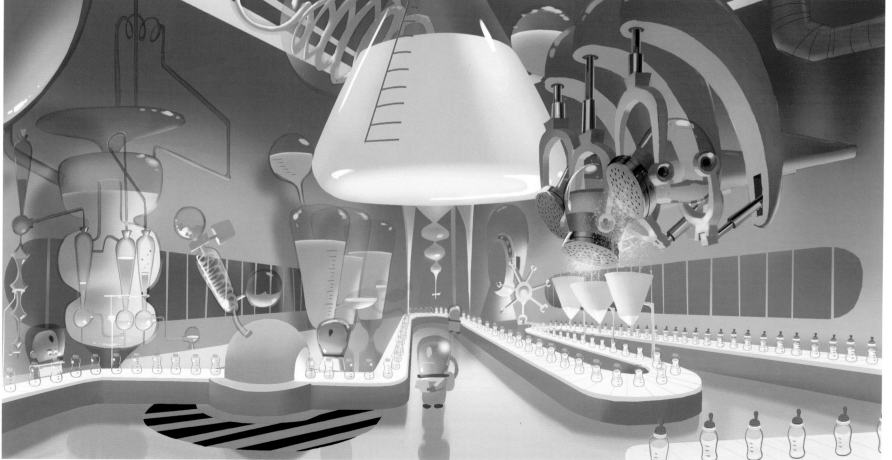

opposite Goro Fudito; *this page* Alex Puvilland

above Alex Puvilland; *opposite top* Chris Brock; *opposite bottom* Ritchie Sacilioc; *page 136 top* Alex Puvilland
page 136 bottom Tom McGrath; *page 137* Max Boas & Raymond Zibach

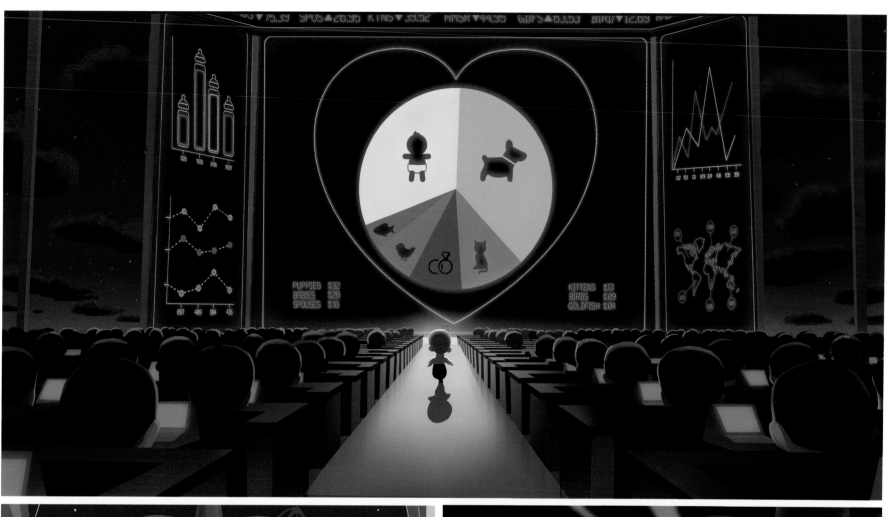

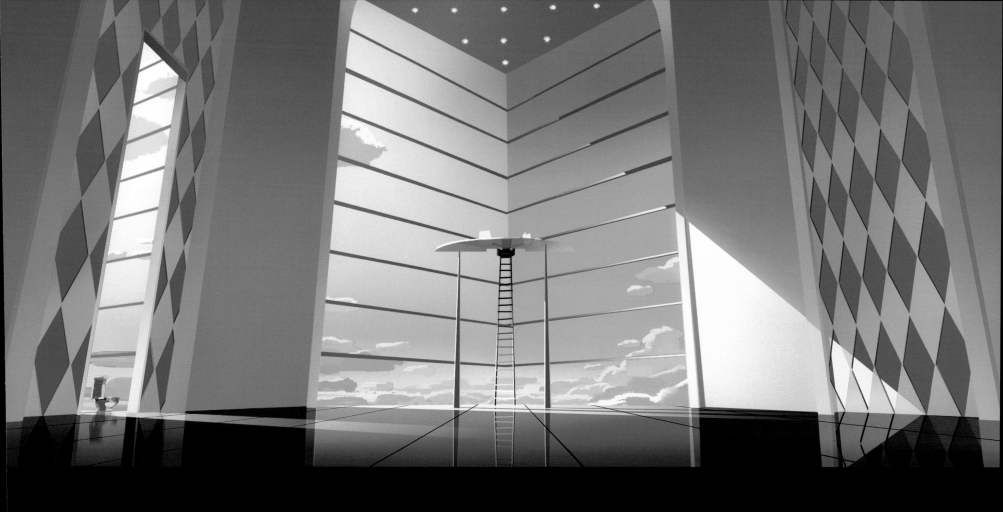

Puppy Co.

Coming up with the right visuals for a corporation that profits from the mass-production of adorable puppies designed to take control of the human population has to be a delight. This highly mechanized factory had to have the garish over-the-top fun of a barn-themed corporate headquarters but also had to convey a certain nostalgic Americana flavor. The result feels like a classic Southern, wood-covered office—the complete opposite of what we see at Baby Corp. Here, the dominant color is red, in contrast to the white we see at the other office.

opposite top, opposite center, and top Andy Schuhler; *opposite bottom* Tom McGrath; *above* Rob Porter
following pages top Ritchie Sacilioc; *following pages bottom* Kenji Ono & Sharon Bridgeman Lukic

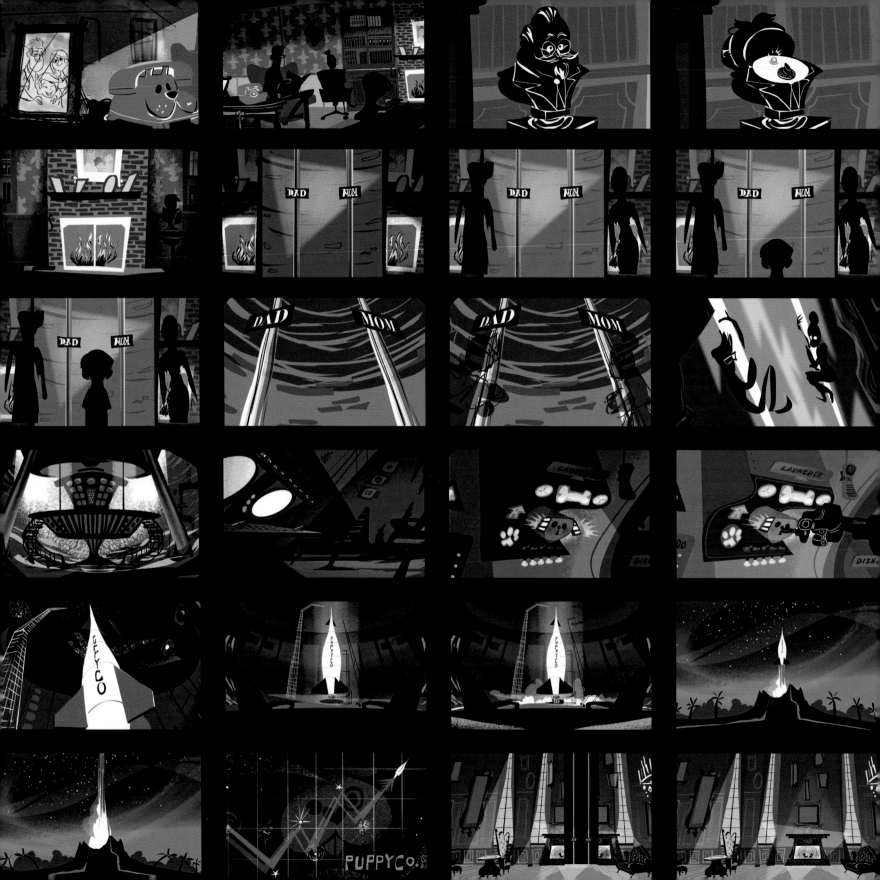

The Airport

Since the house was the setting for the first act of the movie, the filmmakers wanted to make sure they really explored the world outside once Tim and Boss Baby left home. The airport was the perfect setting to make them feel even smaller and more vulnerable in the big world.

"We wanted them to feel lost," recalls director Tom McGrath. "We even designed the costumes as set dressing—everyone is wearing dark suits so that Tim and Boss Baby pop out more. We intentionally didn't include any kids at the airport. We wanted them to feel really small in the big world, so we would root for them even more."

The idea of putting Boss Baby and Tim in a big airport goes back to the first pieces of art generated for the movie pitch by Dan Krull. McGrath says Krull depicted Boss Baby as lost in a sea of adult legs in the airport. "It's really one of the first times that we realize that Boss Baby is just a little baby after all!"

The airport itself has high ceilings and glass walls. Because it's set in a typical US airport of yesteryear, security is very laid-back. "We looked at lots of familiar American airports for inspiration," adds McGrath. "There are even TV sets where you have to put quarters in to watch programs. There's also this notion of how air travel was seen as more of a luxury. People dressed up to get on planes. There was this big movement with the 747 first-class cabins. It was very plush back then. It all seemed very palatial compared to what we have today!"

previous pages Andy Schuhler; *top right* Alex Puvilland
bottom right Glenn Harmon & Javier Recio Garcia

top Dan Krull; *above* Javier Recio Gracia, *opposite* Andy Schuhler

Las Vegas

By the time Boss Baby and Tim arrive in Las Vegas, we are getting further and further removed from the real world. Since the story is told by a not-entirely-reliable narrator (Tim) to his daughter, at this point we get more of a feeling that this is a yarn that's being spun. The visuals get more and more fantastic as well.

"Here we have an impossibly large convention, a little Vegas within Vegas," says production designer David James. "Imagine a wilder, grander version of the Vegas Licensing Show, where the Forever Puppies are being launched in a rocket ship, potentially ending the human race," muses James. "We are becoming untethered by the shackles of logic as we see a wonderland of chasing lights. It's all an incredible, dazzling fantasy of what a child might imagine a pet convention and puppy launch would look like."

these pages Ritchie Sacilioc

PUPPY CONVEYOR BELT.

dog collar

Puppy Co Truck

Sorting Machine

above and opposite top Ritchie Sacilioc; *opposite bottom* Rob Koo; *pages 152–153* Ruben Perez

Anatomy of a Scene

Corner Office, Empty House

Sequence #3100

"It was time to try something completely out of the box."

—*THE BOSS BABY* BY MARLA FRAZEE

It's not often that an animated movie's final scenes crystallize before the rest of the movie. However, when director Tom McGrath and writer Michael McCullers were working on the outline for *The Boss Baby*, they both had a clear idea of how they wanted to resolve the main conflict of the film.

"We wanted to defy the conventional structure that we have seen many times in animated movies," recalls McGrath. "It would have been expected that once the characters defeat the villains and save the parents, they live happily ever after. Michael and I thought it would be great to give Boss Baby and Tim what they want and then for them to realize that's not what they need: They actually need each other."

Sequence 3100, which is titled "Corner Office, Empty House" focuses on this poignant turning point in the lives of both Tim and his strange baby brother. McGrath says he was listening to one of his favorite symphonies when the inspiration for the scene came to him. "I pictured Boss Baby going back to Baby Corp. and receiving a package from Tim," he says. "We wanted to have this beautiful scene in which the characters stop talking and the only things that are driving the movie are the visuals, the acting, the animation, and the music."

The film's creative team used every element in their visual toolbox to pull off this challenging scene. In the beginning of the sequence, both Tim and Boss Baby are in the places where they think they will be the happiest, so they are showered by romantic lighting. "We are showing how great it might have been," explains James. "Of course, they're both far from happy, so as the scene progresses, we transition from later afternoon to early evening to night. As Boss Baby is working late, he receives that letter, and we have this incredible sequence where the entire switchboard—this mission control that calculates all the love everyone is getting—explodes in a shower of sparks as Boss Baby types in this formula: Love + Love + Love = More Love."

The moment that Boss Baby leaves the corporate world, the "tilt-shift" photography style that was used to make the visuals soft, heavenly, and miniature-size reverts back to a more realistic style, echoing his return to reality. When he leaves Baby Corp., it is dawn, the morning of the next day—which ties in neatly with how it all began, as Boss Baby arrived in a taxi in the early morning.

The complexity of the scene also had an impact on all the different story elements that led to it. "We wanted to make sure everything that came before the scene led to this big emotional payoff," notes McGrath. "Sometimes when you tweak some of the elements or the scenes, the ending doesn't work as well. We had to make sure everything that came before Sequence 3100 led up smoothly to this amazing moment. So a lot of love and care went into this scene, which is the pinnacle of Tim and Boss Baby's emotional journey. It brought out the best in every department, and everyone completely rose to the occasion."

opposite Ruben Perez

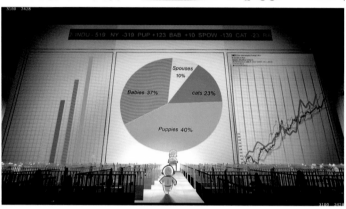

Story

As head of story Ennio Torresan explains, all the details of the sequence had to be just right. "Our director had such a clear vision for this scene that he really imagined the whole movie with this important sequence in mind," says Torresan. "In terms of the story and its emotional impact, it's also one of the most challenging sequences because it's quite heartbreaking, and it's the real finale of the movie."

Almost all the film's story artists worked on this pivotal scene because it had to capture the right mood with the right number of lines. "You have the emotional weight of what Boss Baby and Tim are feeling, as well as some comedic elements, since the baby workers are sent in to clean up the house of Boss's belongings," notes Torresan. "There's also the business with the beads, which symbolize the love between the two brothers, and which Tim gives to Boss Baby as a gift. The sequence is about four minutes long, but we went back to it over and over again throughout the length of the production. Every time we had a screening, we would go back and fine-tune this scene because it reveals the emotional core of *Boss Baby*."

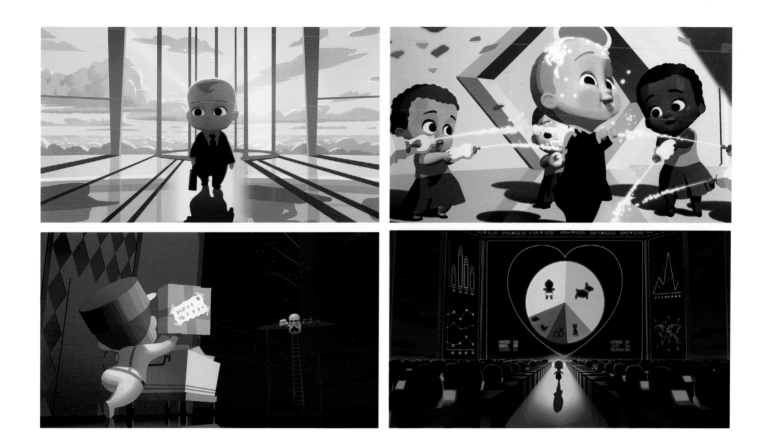

Color Keys

Production designer David James also calls the scene the crescendo of the movie. "We've been building up to this moment," he notes. "The whole premise of the film—the fact that there is enough love for everybody—becomes clear when Tim sends Boss Baby those beads [that represent the love available in a family] and writes him this memo, which is also a callback to the beginning of the film. This is when Boss Baby throws off the shackles of corporate existence and leaves Baby Corp. to join his brother."

Throughout the scene, the only words the audience hears are the heartfelt words of a seven-year-old boy who misses his brother. In the letter, he repeats the lines that Boss Baby told him at the beginning of the movie: "Every morning when you wake up, I'll be there. Every Christmas party, I will be there. You and I will always be brothers." This time around, the words mean something entirely different. They point to the promise of their future lives together.

"It's a beautifully emotional scene, and our biggest challenge was figuring out the best way to make it poetic and simple," says producer Ramsey Naito. "Most of the time, less is more, and you have to emote through visuals instead of words. It's all about figuring out the right equation, and you need to allow your team to iterate until you get the best result."

opposite top left Tom McGrath; *opposite bottom right* Ennio Torresan
top right and bottom left Ruben Perez; *bottom right* Alex Puvilland

Previsualization

One of the most unusual aspects of Sequence 3100 is that director Tom McGrath had actually boarded it six years ago. "It was a very personal scene for him, so he had already done a lot of work on it, even before he had a script," says Kent Seki, the film's head of layout.

Seki says the previs team had to pull out all the stops because the scene had over seven different lighting set ups as well as several complicated cinematic elements. "One of the big concepts for the film was that we used tilt-shift photography with the crazy depth of field when we are at Baby Corp.," says Seki. "As the film progresses and Boss Baby finally realizes that he wants to be part of the family, we move away from tilt-shift and go for deep focus."

When Boss Baby gets the letter from Tim and dumps what seems like an infinite number of beads on the table, the previs team had to use 3-D to make the scene deeper. "We were also doing this camera dolly effect, which is reminiscent of the effect Hitchcock uses in *Vertigo*," recalls Seki. "You change the focal length and move the camera to compensate for it, creating this effect that the whole world is changing around Boss Baby. It's a great cinematic experience, and it really pushed us in terms of the amount of performance we were trying out in the previs stage."

Modeling and Surfacing

Creating this palpable sense of loss was also high on the visual effects team's list of priorities. "We worked closely with Tom and David to go through all the items in the house that would reflect this loss," says senior visual effects supervisor Tony K. Williams. "There were specific items in the house, such as paintings and photographs, that were the most emotional, as we see the little helpers in hazmat suits deconstructing Boss's bedroom. They're disassembling the crib and carrying it out of the house and taking it to Baby Corp."

The big challenge for the modeling and surfacing team was selecting assets that would be quickly identifiable by the audience. "You see the mattress or Boss's teddy bear all being moved out," explains Williams. "They're removing all traces of the baby, so Tim is completely bewildered. As adults, we have moments in our lives when we look back and think, 'Did I do the right thing?' and 'Was it the right decision?' They leave you with this ambiguous feeling. However, kids and adults are going to look at this scene in completely different ways, and that's what we like to see."

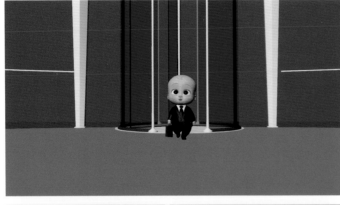

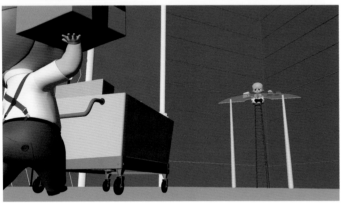
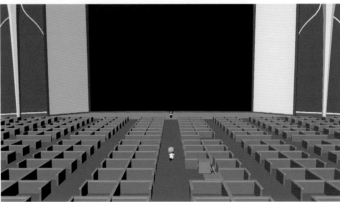

Rigging and Animation

The animation team went into this sequence knowing that they needed to sharpen their emotional "teeth" and deliver performances that would keep the audience engaged and invested in the characters. As head of animation Carlos Puertolas explains, "Our goal was to create performances that would keep the audience on the verge of tears but that also uplifted them during the second half of the sequence."

The team of fourteen animators led by Puertolas worked on the scenes for five to seven weeks each. The sequence was so extensive that it was divided into two parts, and two supervisors oversaw it. Rather than breaking it up by the number of shots, the work was divided by the two characters—Boss Baby and Tim.

Puertolas points out that one of the most challenging aspects of this sequence was finding the right performance for Tim and Boss Baby. "If the emotion was pushed too far, it could damage the sincerity of the scene; if it was kept too subtle, the audience might not fully connect and empathize with the characters," he notes. "We tried out different acting approaches and levels of emotion until we found the perfect balance."

At this point in the movie, the team was very familiar with the rigs and how much they could manipulate them. "Luckily, we didn't really encounter any technical challenges, which left us in the perfect situation to be able to fully concentrate on the acting," Puertolas says.

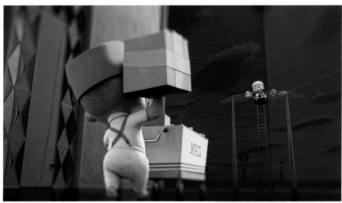
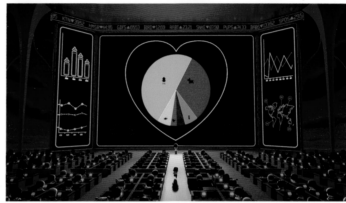

Lighting and Visual Effects

Head of lighting Rajarajan Ramakrishnan says his team listened closely to the film's director when he told them that this sequence was the most important story moment in the film. The primary task was to light the entire sequence to convey the rich transformation Boss Baby and Tim go through. "We needed to make the subtle character performances come through the various lighting scenarios," he says. "Even though there were emotionally low moments, we needed to stay away from being dark and ominous."

One of their big challenges was to make sure the characters read well against the colorful, reflective environments. "In many cases, we were lighting them in back-light conditions and still allowing the mixed emotions to come through clearly," says Ramakrishnan. "The various sets and different lighting conditions, along with the tilt-shift effect, were really cool for any lighter to play with. The entire team had a great time pulling this off."